Dinosaur Hunters

by Leonie Bennett

Editorial consultant: Mitch Cronick

Copyright © **ticktock Entertainment Ltd 2006**
First published in Great Britain in 2006 by **ticktock Media Ltd.,**
Unit 2, Orchard Business Centre, North Farm Road, Tunbridge Wells, Kent TN2 3XF

We would like to thank: Shirley Bickler and Suzanne Baker

ISBN 1 86007 967 9 pbk
Printed in China

Picture credits
t=top, b=bottom, c=centre, l-left, r=right, OFC= outside front cover
Corbis: Page 13. Dinosaur artwork: ticktock Media Ltd.

CONTENTS

What did dinosaur hunters look like?   4

How big were they?   6

Dinosaur food   8

Hunting   10

Tyrannosaurus rex   12

Deinonychus   14

Velociraptor   16

Segnosaurus   18

Coelophysis   20

Yes or no? Talking about dinosaurs   22

Activities   24

What did dinosaur hunters look like?

They had big heads.

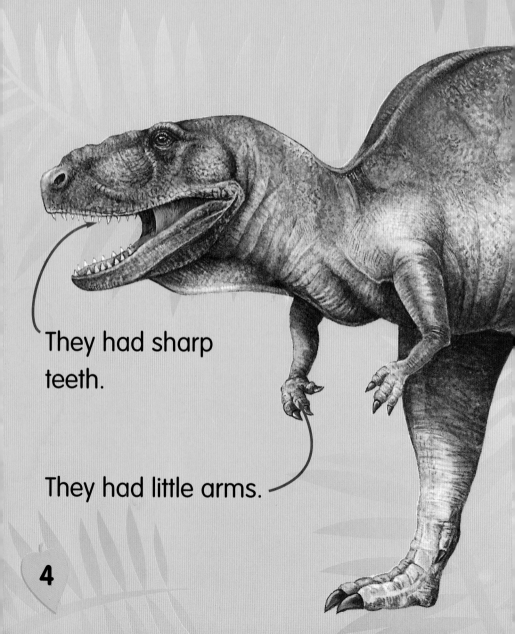

They had sharp teeth.

They had little arms.

Giganotosaurus

They had long tails.

They had long
legs.

5

How big were they?

Some dinosaur hunters were small.

Compsognathus

Dinosaur size

Man

This dinosaur was as small as a cat.

Some dinosaur hunters were big.

Allosaurus

Dinosaur size

Man

This dinosaur was nine metres long.

Dinosaur food

Dinosaur hunters ate other animals.

Dinosaur hunters were meat-eaters.

Tyrannosaurus rex

Some dinosaur hunters ate other dinosaurs.

Some dinosaur hunters
ate other animals.

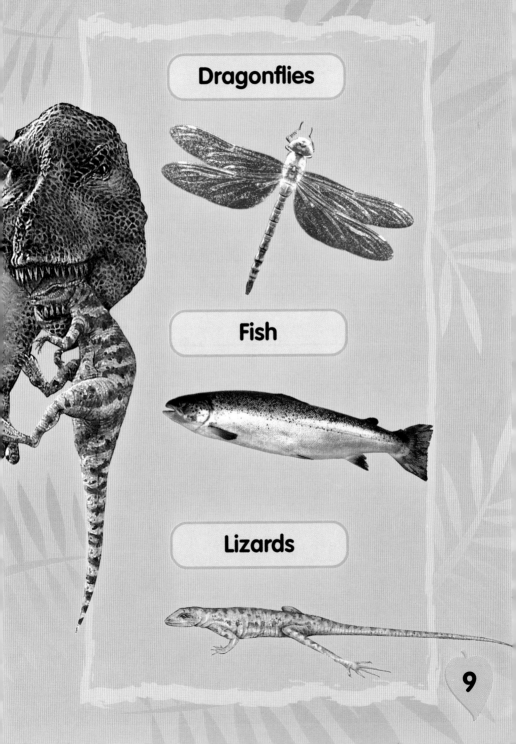

Dragonflies

Fish

Lizards

Hunting

Some dinosaurs hunted alone.

Dilophosaurus

Some dinosaurs hunted in a group.

They used their sharp teeth.

They used their
big claws.

Deinonychus

Tyrannosaurus rex
(tie-ran-o-sor-us rex)

Tyrannosaurus rex ate other dinosaurs.

It had big teeth.

T. rex

T. rex means 'lizard king'.

This is a T. rex fossil.

Dinosaur size

Man

A fossil is a very old bone that has turned into rock.

Deinonychus (die-non-ee-cus)

This dinosaur ran very fast.

It ran after its prey.

It had very big claws.

It was very fierce.

Dinosaur size

Man

14

Deinonychus

This dinosaur's name means 'terrible claw'.

Velociraptor
(vel-oss-ee-rap-tor)

This dinosaur had feathers like a bird.

This dinosaur's name means 'speedy thief'.

Velociraptor

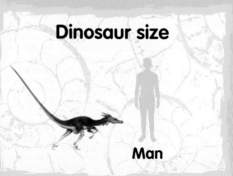

Dinosaur size

Man

It had a long tail.

It had a very big claw on its back foot.

17

Segnosaurus (seg-no-sor-us)

This dinosaur's name means 'slow lizard'.

Segnosaurus

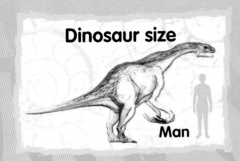

Dinosaur size

Man

It had feathers like a bird.

It had long arms.

It had very long claws.

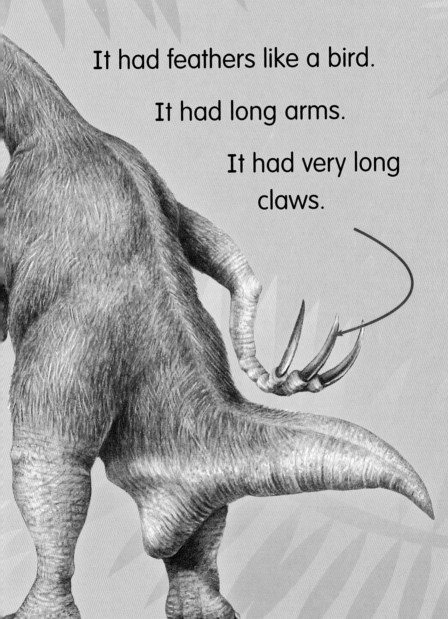

19

Coelophysis (see-lo-fie-sis)

These dinosaurs ate lizards and small dinosaurs.

They lived in big groups.

20

Coelophysis

They had small arms and
long legs.

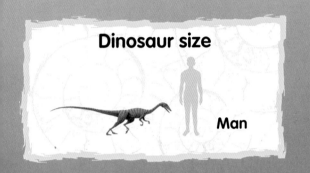

Dinosaur size

Man

21

Yes or no?
Talking about dinosaurs

Dinosaur hunters had little heads.

Yes or no?

Tyrannosaurus rex had big teeth.

Yes or no?

Deinonychus means 'terrible teeth'.

Yes or no?

Segnosaurus
had feathers.

Yes or no?

Would you like to meet
Tyrannosaurus rex?
Why or why not?

Activities

What did you think of this book?

 Brilliant   **Good**   **OK**

Which page did you like best? Why?

• • • • • • • • • • • • • •

Which of these dinosaurs is the smallest? Which is the biggest?

Tyrannosaurus rex • Compsognathus • Velociraptor

• • • • • • • • • • • • • •

Invent a dinosaur! Draw a big picture and label it. Use these words:

arms • claws • legs • tail • teeth

• • • • • • • • • • • • • •

Who is the author of this book? Have you read *Dinosaur Plant-eaters* by the same author?